The Tao Of Emotion

Book One, Awaken

By Gabriel Deeds

Illustrations by Robin Thompson

Lynn Valley Literary Society

Also by Gabriel Deeds,

The Tao Of Emotion series,

Book Two - First Steps

Book Three - The Long Road

www.taoofemotion.com

Contents

www.taoofemotion.com

Introduction

Most of us at some point ask, "Why? What is this life all about?" All the blood, sweat and tears, the sheer effort and pain in just getting by. Why?

Answers are few, but every now and then a piece clicks into place and we go "Aha!" As a species we have some ugly habits but we can also shine. When one of us discovers a piece of life's puzzle, there is a strong need to share. What's the point of discovering something amazing if you can't share it? After all, what are we without each other?

Ultimately it is how we interact with each other that determines the quality of our lives. The choices that we make can bring fulfilment and purpose or, frustration and misery. It is vital therefore that those choices should be conscious and informed and yet that is rarely the case.

All human interactions have a common thread running through them; they are full to overflowing with glorious emotion. We are an emotional species. A staggering 80% of our behaviour is controlled by emotion! So it seems obvious that to make conscious life choices we would need awareness and knowledge of our emotions, yet we know little about them. Our own emotions are a mystery to us!

This lack of emotional awareness blights every aspect of our lives, relationships, career and family life. It stunts us spiritually, intellectually and physically. It turns our world into a self made hell on earth in which we toil, enslaved, oblivious to our own miserable plight. We have no real knowledge of who we are.

The tools are there, the knowledge exists and the time is right. We are tired and weary, ripe for change. More people than ever are ready, even desperate for the next level.

So let's get started.

Nothing much has changed

Chapter 1 - The Human Dilemma

For thousands of years humanity survived without self awareness or anything but basic intelligence. We not only survived, we came to dominate the planet even driving our competitors into extinction.

We rose up on a potent mixture of instinct, teamwork and ruthless violence. Nothing much has changed. Survival of the fittest was the name of the game and it was the *only* game in town. Our existence was, is, dominated by the unconscious mind. Our survival, reproduction, social interactions, all driven by the unconscious! Self awareness and higher consciousness were unknown. Intelligence was rudimentary at best, just enough brains to avoid poisoning ourselves or to avoid offending the dominant male.

Intelligence evolved making an already powerful species unstoppable. Some individuals

Consciousness evolving.

were able to assess and cope with fluid situations not covered by the unconscious script. They prospered and consciousness evolved. Consciousness and awareness of self and how self relates to the bigger picture became important. An individual endowed with these traits had the ability to improve status and circumstances, a distinct advantage.

When resources are scarce it is the individuals with lower status that suffer the most. This is still a basic truth today. You don't want to be at the bottom and you don't really want to be at the top. The top is a dangerous and lonely place to be, the top is where everybody paints their bulls eye. Ideally we aim to be somewhere in the middle, cushioned at both ends of the food chain.

To assess and successfully manipulate complex family and tribal politics requires something more than the unconscious mind can provide. The unconscious deals successfully with

The unconscious has no concept of time

most of our day to day needs and their corresponding behaviours; however the conscious mind is good at dealing with dynamic, fluid and unique situations. It's not glamorous, but this is where consciousness evolved.

So human kind covered the earth, breeding, fighting and spreading until the only competition was other people. It should be noted at this point that the happiness of the individual was not exactly high on the unconscious agenda. The concept of happiness is inconceivable to the dominant unconscious, it is unable to conceptualise. The concept of time is also inconceivable. To the unconscious everything is the same today as it was 10,000 years ago. Your unconscious lives in a time warp, it is important that you remember this.

Our consciousness blossomed; we began to express our new found self awareness in different ways. People painted on walls and on themselves,

Spirituality verses religion

they had leisure time and began to question the stars and look for meaning and purpose within their existence. The concept of creation and a creator arose. Promising? Perhaps.

Inevitably our fledgling Spirituality was hijacked by the unconscious. Religious persecution, pogroms, purges and inquisitions have been responsible for more death and suffering than any other form of human discrimination.

What happened? How could a thing like spirituality be twisted in such a way? There is more.

From our intellect came science, medicine and technology and yet somehow this led to new and more terrible weapons. From a simple rock thrown in anger, to neutron bombs, war and conflict have always driven science. There is nothing quite like an arms race to promote science and technology and so intellect is also corrupted.

Spirituality is twisted into religion

Physically we are bigger, stronger and faster than we have ever been. The epitome of physical perfection is represented in the Olympic Games. The ultimate competition is based entirely on martial arts!

Spirituality, intellect, the physical aspect, all corrupted but by what? Somehow, no matter how advanced we become, we seem unable to truly benefit from our efforts. The world should be a better place. Our lives should be more fulfilling and happier than they are? Why is there so much war, famine and disease? Why do 30,000 children a day die of neglect? Why is the world so unhappy?

Our mental, physical and spiritual endeavours are **all** influenced, twisted in fact, by a powerful force, emotion. However emotion is merely a symptom of a far greater force, the unconscious mind. Emotion is the tool by which the unconscious dominates our behaviour and rules 80% of our lives.

Something is missing?

Even in the affluent west peace and happiness are scare commodities. In many ways the individual living in modern society is more miserable and wretched than the so called primitive bushman. Suicide, divorce, alcohol and drug abuse are spiralling epidemics, the scourge of civilisation.

Today, we all feel a lacking in our lives, something is desperately wrong, something is missing. We have just enough consciousness to realise this but insufficient self awareness to understand the root cause.

Actually it's not that there is something missing, it's that there is more going on within us than we are aware of. That's a big surprise for most of us, addicted as we are, to our intellect and ego.

There is a fundamental clash between the ancient unconscious order and our new emerging higher consciousness. Humanity is caught between an immovable object and an unstoppable force.

The old unconscious system is our default setting. It's sole objective is survival of the fittest, it's main goal is conflict. The unconscious naturally creates an arena for conflict. Survival yes, but survival of the fittest. Survival of the species not merely the individual and survival at a terrible cost.

The unconscious wants gladiators not Enlightened beings! Happiness? Peace? Fulfilment? What are they to the unconscious? It cares only that we compete and survive. It does not do abstract concepts like happiness and peace.

Our behaviours and unconscious thought processes have evolved to create an environment which promotes conflict. Conflict in all its forms is the life blood of our unconscious existence. Children at the breast compete for milk. They compete for mum's attention and they struggle to impress dad. We do whatever it takes to stay within the protective umbrella of family and tribe where the odds of survival are significantly better. We come to conflict early and we rarely give it up.

We struggle to build empires and then we struggle to overthrow them. We are driven to perpetual strife by our own unconscious default settings. We behave like mindless, expendable pawns in an endless cycle of conflict and suffering.

Now, this worked beautifully for thousands of years. Conflict and suffering grew at a most gratifying rate. That is self evident. No matter what lofty goals we foolishly believed that we had set for ourselves. Communism, fascism, capitalism, racial or religious purity, material success, self defence, freedom, all grist to the mill. It doesn't matter one bit, the unconscious imperative remains the same, to compete and to survive.

Somebody will eventually dominate, but winning is not the real objective. The winner instantly becomes a target so that the whole cycle can continue. Ask any President or Prime Minister, any leader soon learns that the honeymoon period is all too short. No matter how gifted, charismatic or brutal, it's just a question of time before the

Conflict rocks!

mob turns on you and tears you to bits.

Each one of us carries this code of conflict within and naturally we bring it to the world we live in. It permeates every aspect of your life excluding the possibility of happiness. So don't be surprised when you hear the news and feel depressed. Don't be surprised if you find happiness hard to find. We reap what we have sown with such unconscious abandon. As my niece would say, "Karma!" Unconscious emotional behaviour has painfully real and unavoidable consequences.

As we became more self aware, we came to want more than endless conflict. Great teachers regularly appear speaking of love, compassion and self fulfilment. Of course we ridicule, persecute and even kill them. If that doesn't work we slavishly follow them and corrupt their teachings. What could be more threatening to the unconscious regime?

21

Unconscious behaviour has consequences!

Somehow though, their ideas took root, some resonating truth was apparent to our growing consciousness. We began to see at least the possibility of a better way.

We are evolving, or trying to but the old unconscious order reigns supreme. It laughs at our vain attempts to find happiness. It only cares about our physical survival and it is not remotely interested in happiness. Naturally, we are unhappy because happy folks don't fight. Happy people are useless to the ruling unconscious!

Surely though, we are conscious beings, surely we are in charge of our own lives? We like to think so but in fact around 80% of our day to day behaviour is determined by the unconscious mind. Our enemies, friends and lovers, our careers, passions and secret fears, even our passing moods are all dictated by the unconscious. This is a scientific fact! We are not the conscious beings that we fondly believe ourselves to be!

Everything in our lives is secretly pre-programmed to create conflict. Our efforts to find happiness are constantly undermined by our own invisible unconscious desire for conflict. This realisation was a dreadful shock to me but it made a terrible sense. I knew it was true, I could **feel** it. As I realised, the truth of it gripped me intellectually, spiritually, physically and crucially, emotionally. I recognised the truth as only a human being can.

I was devastated when I realised the nature and extent of the suffering that we all endure, especially as children! All children are subjected to this horror. Their innocence and vulnerability twisted by the unconscious world order. They are moulded from innocents into scarred, cynical competitors imbued with the ridiculous notion that they in themselves are not good enough, that they must fight to win their place in this cauldron of conflict that we call home.

Such mindless cruelty, without any real purpose other than to promote the cycle of suffering and create an arena for gladiators to fight in. The strong survive and flourish while the weak wither and perish? Is that really what we want for ourselves and for our children? If the answer is no, then we have work to do.

This was a valid approach pre-consciousness but is completely inappropriate for sentient beings. But this is not something that we do consciously as a matter of choice. The unconscious automatic pilot removes choice because choice means deliberation and costs time. To our primitive unconscious this is an unacceptable risk. That millisecond could be the difference between life and death.

In our well ordered suburban existence the life and death imperative is difficult to comprehend. We delude ourselves into thinking that we are masters of the universe, a higher form of life when actually the truth is that we are

Brothers in arms

dominated by a primeval unconscious of which we are barely aware.

Realising this fact alone is crucial if we are to break the cycle of suffering and evolve. In realising the true nature of your own dilemma you also realise how much we all have in common. We share this most intimate experience if we could only see it. Suddenly our competitors became fellow slaves, all of us tormented and frustrated by an outdated unconscious.

Our suffering unites us in a common bond forged in agony. We are brothers and sisters in arms, not competitors. The enemy is ignorance of our dominant unconscious and the emotional mechanisms by which it controls us.

We know that we are in a state of disharmony, that is painfully obvious, but we don't know how or why. We have outgrown the mindless regime of the unconscious but because we are unaware of it's dominating influence and the means by which it controls us we are trapped

The Universe will not let us go

in misery between our growing consciousness and the unconscious. No wonder that our lives are so uncomfortable!

The individual cannot choose consciousness until first understanding the unconscious and the role of emotion in our day to day behaviour. The most devout monk, the most intellectual scientist can make only limited progress without first understanding the unconscious. We are stunted by our ignorance of ourselves.

The first step is to realise the nature of this, our human dilemma. Become aware of it and be amazed by the power and pervasive subtlety of the unconscious mind. Admire it and recognise it's achievement. It is not our enemy; it brought us to where we are. We are simply outgrowing it.

No matter who we are or how wise, this realisation is the starting point. Now we can journey forward instead of going around in circles trapped in a vicious cycle of ignorance and suffering.

The true self is shrouded in mystery

To know yourself you must study your unconscious which obscures who you really are. The phoney projection that you show the world is merely an illusion, an elaborate, unconscious fabrication. Through it you not only deceive the world, you deceive yourself. Your true self is shrouded in mystery. You do not know who you really are and therefore you can never truly love yourself or anybody else. All of this would be impossible; you simply do not know who you are.

To realise this is to realise your own purpose in this life. Naturally you must get to know yourself. This is the riddle of life set us by a wise Universe for it is in the pursuit of self knowledge that we find peace and fulfilment. This is where we find Divinity and peace. This is work enough for anyone, a true quest, fit for heroes.

However we rarely see our own lives from this perspective, we have little real idea of the intrinsic value of the individual. We pay the notion

There are none so blind....

lip service but it fails to impact our behaviour in any meaningful way. We live buried and distracted by the false, competitive realities of our unconscious, emotion filled world. To deny yourself is foolish and will only send you back to the mindless cycle of suffering from whence you came.

Sadly that is what most people choose to do. There are none so blind as those who do not wish to see. We are frightened, scared of change, scared of progress, even scared of a glorious future! Most people merely exist, suffering shadows of who they could be. They never realise their true potential, they don't know how.

There is a lot of anxiety and confusion surrounding the subject. We prefer to follow rather than lead, stepping up is risky and for what? Where will it take us, will we be any better off? The unconscious makes us afraid.

The unconscious does not encourage self examination. Change is not something that we enjoy and this will be reflected in our feelings. This manifests itself in many ways,

"I don't have time," "If it ain't broke don't fix it," "Nobody else is doing this," "It's always been this way," "Who am I to change things?" "Psychobabble!" Or we simply stay immersed in modern minutia, clinging to our distractions and addictive illusions, too anxious and afraid to look up and wonder.

Most people are hiding themselves in work, relationships and addictions. Anything but face the reality of their own personal responsibility.

This is not down to God. We can't blame anyone no matter how abused we have been. It's down to us, individually, personally, finally, and that scares us. Of course it does, this is a scary business.

However it is our failure to engage and our dependence on the unconscious, the devil that we know, that generates most of our suffering. That suffering grows and reaches a tipping point. We begin to seek other ways driven by suffering. That is the nature and purpose of suffering. We are not supposed to merely endure it, to become accustomed to it. We are supposed to change our ways.

We have moved on but until we come to grips with our own unconscious and the emotional mechanism by which it controls us we will be stunted. Spiritually, intellectually and physically, we will never attain our true potential. Our best endeavours will always be twisted and bent to the will of the unconscious. Conflict and strife will always prevail.

Why?

Chapter 2 - Why Are We Here?

We fear change and yet we also fear that there is no purpose to our existence. Ironically that double fear actually makes change inevitable as we seek meaning in our lives. We are unique, intelligent, sentient beings capable of determining our own destiny. How could such a being have no purpose?

That horrible little question, "Why?" has haunted us since we first looked up at the stars and wondered. Could it all be just an evolutionary quirk, mere biology? Somehow that thought fills us with dread.

It is this fear that leads many of us into religion (as opposed to spirituality.) Formerly the opiate of the people, religion has been replaced by more modern opiates. Materialism, relationships and work for example, but even these are insufficient to dull the pain of an unfulfilled existence.

This fundamental state of disharmony and the consequences that derive from it should motivate us to seek change. We are in transition, we are **NOT** supposed to endure suffering or get used to it as some would have us believe.

"Toughen up!" "Life's a bitch and then you die!" We are taught to accept and tolerate our state of ignorance and our consequent suffering. Then there is "faith", which soon becomes corrupted into inaction. God and not man will take care of it if we just have faith. We fear progress preferring our miserable little fur lined ruts to the prospect of change. This is how the unconscious enslaves us. It is so much easier to do nothing, to complain and to blame and bring to heel those who question and seek more. Their very existence is a challenge, an implied criticism to those who do nothing.

Our purpose is clear. It is to discover self, to fathom the true nature of the whole being including the mysterious unconscious. In this way we can reconstruct ourselves consciously ascending to our true destiny. We can meet ourselves and in so doing meet God at home, within us.

This is what it means to be re-born or rather consciously reconstructed. First, however you must de-construct yourself in order to properly understand who you are. Then, as you examine each piece you can decide which ones are working to your satisfaction and which ones need to be discarded or repaired.

It is in accepting personal responsibility for this work that we change not only ourselves but the very nature of the world that we share together. **Everything** else flows from this. This is the conscious foundation that a sentient being requires to find harmony. Relationships, career, recreation, health and happiness all flow from here. Only then can we break the cycle of suffering and move on to the next level, wherever it takes us.

Direct your own destiny

This is how we become masters of our own destiny, our true purpose in this life.

There are no guarantees, no maps, no real control. This is the ultimate exploration, the final frontier and it scares the hell out of us. The unconscious whispers in our ears sowing doubt, raising fears and so we simply don't go. We stay behind and suffer, generation after generation teaching our children the same old dogmatic rubbish.

This is the ultimate personal responsibility and we would rather stick pins in our eyes than begin such a daunting journey. So the Universe cranks up the heat, our suffering increases. We lurch forward a few faltering steps and then give up and return to what we know until, once again, it becomes unbearable. Talk about doing things the hard way!

We seem unable to perceive the nature of our own plight. We just aren't getting it collectively. The Tao Of Emotion is, above all, designed to offer a fresh perspective on our false reality. Our illusions can no longer sustain us. Once we *truly* realise the nature of our own dilemma we will simply be unable to endure it any longer. At this crucial point we are very vulnerable. We need the guidance of common, shared experience. The knowledge that others have gone before, that there is a Way, that it can be done, must be done. This too is the role of The Tao Of Emotion. We can travel together.

Self Knowledge

Self knowledge has long been recognised as the key to Enlightenment. "Know thyself and thou shall know all the mysteries of the gods and of the universe." (Inscribed on the gateway to the Oracle at Delphi.) Buddha, Jesus, Lao Tzu, modern science (Freud and Jung,) all agree that to "Know thyself," is to fulfil human destiny.

Sounds great, but what does that mean to the individual struggling to pay bills and raise kids? First of all, you have to want change, no easy thing. You may consciously decide that you do want change but you must realise that your dominant unconscious does not!

The unconscious is a bit like a hostile witness in the courtroom. You might think that it is there to help but actually it is undermining and obstructing everything that you consciously do. I find that the easiest way to understand how the unconscious works is to recognise this hostility and to ask the judge (your own consciousness) for permission to treat the unconscious as hostile.

A witness may be deemed hostile when, *"The witness' testimony is clearly prejudiced."* The unconscious seeks control and avoids change, it *is* biased. There is a clear conflict between conscious and unconscious. This adversarial approach creates a fresh perspective and objectivity and therefore allows for a conscious judgement. You can objectively stand outside yourself and regard your own unconscious emotions almost like a third party, before you act.

Realising the nature of the relationship between the unconscious and the conscious you and treating the unconscious as "hostile" is a very different approach. It allows you to frame the intangible unconscious in a familiar way, as an opponent. This denies the unconscious one of it's primary weapons, invisibility. It is very hard to combat an opponent that you cannot see and impossible to fight one of which you are completely unaware!

It's like waking up at night and realising that something is wrong in the house. Perhaps you hear a strange noise or hear the dog growl, suddenly you are awake. You immediately begin to deal with the situation, assess the threat and examine your options. Even better if you can nudge the person next to you and share the problem.

Do you put your head under the pillow and hope the problem will go away? Of course not! Recognising a problem you accept responsibility for it and begin to deal with it. You might call the police or grab a bat; as soon as a problem is identified human beings immediately begin to seek solutions.

Of course the unconscious is not actually an enemy. It's role is to help us to survive but it is slow to change and we are outgrowing it. Our world is no longer filled with life and death situations. It's time to realise that our current unconscious default settings are a problem for our evolving consciousness. Transition is what we are after not a complete break.

For example, a modern airliner is almost impossible for a human pilot to fly. There are too many forces at work, too many tasks that must be addressed simultaneously. The pilot would be overwhelmed and exhausted, so she has computers and onboard systems to do most of the work. However the pilot is in charge.

A human life is similar but in this case the pilot is ornamental. The pilot likes to think that she is in charge but actually she is completely dependent on the machine, she just doesn't realise it. Blindly flying around in circles she knows that something is wrong but the auto pilot keeps saying,

"Just sit back and let me take care of it."
Everything seems normal but she is unhappy because deep down she knows that she's supposed to be in charge. There is somewhere she's supposed to be and the fuel gauge is creeping towards empty. Life is a finite resource. She's scared to take the stick or even read the manual in case she crashes. We can't live like that and expect to find any peace.

It might not seem like it but actually we are all trapped on the horns of the same unconscious dilemma, you are not alone on this trip. We all have the same work to do and using a common process, (The Tao Of Emotion,) brings us together making us immeasurably more powerful.

This sharing, processing approach is familiar to us and that brings comfort in a stressful, radically different situation. It offers the comfort of communion and shared experience. As a species human beings are capable of amazing feats especially when they work together against a common foe. The unconscious denies us this collective resource isolating us as individuals and setting us against each other. Working together towards a common goal, anything is possible.

So we have become aware of the problem, we have the unconscious at the end of our flashlight, what are we going to do with it? The missing key to self knowledge is found in a most unpromising place, it is found within our emotions. It is through emotion that the unconscious is able to dominate our behaviour and create the self made hell that we inhabit. It is through the study and understanding of our emotion that we will escape our unconscious master and find true self knowledge.

Chapter 3 - Emotion

Let's start with how we behave on a day to day basis.

Fact - it is our own behaviour that fills our lives and this world with conflict and suffering. It's not God, it's not the boss at work or the country next door or the damned sun worshippers. We are personally responsible.

Fact - 80% of our behaviour is based on unconscious not conscious thought. Freud expressed this in his third blow to the human ego. We are not the conscious beings that we believe ourselves to be.

The first blow came from Copernicus who proved that the earth was not the centre of the universe. The truth is that we exist on a round, blue rock, spinning around the sun in a galaxy hurtling through the void at unimaginable speeds. Gulp!

The second blow came with Darwin's theory of evolution. The establishment, especially the church, reacted badly to simple truth. How could God's chosen ones be related to monkeys?

Then Freud waded in with the third blow to the human ego, that we aren't even conscious beings but unconscious beings! How could humanity, with all of its knowledge and sophistication be dominated by unconscious, emotional behaviour? Most people are not even aware of Freud never mind how their lives are effected by their own unconscious emotion.

How long until this truth is accepted and understood? Freud's blow is the one that most effects us as individuals. It is disturbing, even offensive and so naturally it will take longer to become accepted as truth, for truth it is. Feel it for yourself, humans have that capacity. This ability is another defining feature of humanity. Use it.

Emotion rules our world!

It is important that you realise this truth at least intellectually, the rest will follow. I find that it explains a great deal about the world we live in. Our persistent inability to find happiness and fulfilment and our distinct lack of purpose can now be explained. Many of us sense that something is wrong and now we can define it. That in itself is a real achievement.

Even semi conscious beings could never be happy dominated by a system based on unconscious emotion designed for dumb brutes. A system that generates conflict creating a survival of the fittest regime is not fit for sentient beings. Of course we are unhappy. Emotion rules us, emotion rules our world.

We are ready to move on but until we understand where we come from and who we are, we cannot proceed. We will always end up back where we started, frustrated, unhappy and confused. This is where our own unconscious wants us. In a twisted way, this is where we are comfortable. This is how we evolved into such a combative, argumentative species. This is where our biological success came from.

It is the study of our emotions that will allow us to understand the nature of our human dilemma realising true self knowledge. The emotional aspect is without doubt the least understood, it is also the most powerful, by far. Yet, amazingly, most of us are just plain ignorant when it comes to our emotions.

The mental, physical and spiritual aspects of humanity are well recognised. We accept their value even dedicating our lives to their study. Then we have emotion, the poor relative of self knowledge. As our weakest aspect by far it is also an amazing opportunity. This is fertile ground that has never been tilled before. Those who take on the job face a daunting task, true, but they also face unimaginable rewards. This is like discovering a new continent, a new, undeveloped world.

As our least developed aspect emotion holds us back on **every** level. Intellect, spirituality, even the physical aspect cannot be separated from emotion. Emotion in the form of stress kills millions of us every year and makes billions more unhappy. The influence of our recognised aspects is minimal compared to emotion in terms of how it directly effects our behaviour and the quality of our lives.

The most brilliant scientist may be lonely and miserable. The most enlightened monk may be beset with self doubt and lust. The greatest athlete may never reach his full potential without real emotional self awareness and the confidence and self love that comes with it.

We attempt life without a secure emotional foundation and so all that we do is undermined ultimately re-enforcing the overwhelming illusion that our unconscious behaviour creates. Yet there is no class on emotion, no instruction manual, no treatment. We tend to ignore or even suppress our emotion. Most of us don't even realise that our

Emotionally we are all children

emotional ignorance is a problem. Yet we live daily with the consequences, from domestic disputes to world war. We completely fail to make the connection between emotional ignorance and our suffering.

Generation after generation unerringly repeats the same old mistakes. Our parents and teachers were as ignorant as we are. So how then could we be anything but emotionally inept? Emotion is not seen as important; it's just a fact of life like your period or losing your hair. Emotionally we are all children!

Every emotion is a response to stimuli. For example a threat breeds fear, anger and then violence, fight or flight. That predetermined, emotional response comes from our unconscious perception of what threatens us.

How you perceive threats will depend on how you feel about yourself in relation to the people around you. Carnivorous predators aside, the threats, real or imagined, that we face today are primarily generated by our human interactions. What we broadly refer to as "bad" behaviour, the root of our suffering, comes from,

1. Our insecurities and inadequacies.
2. Our consequent competitive nature.

The greater your self awareness and self esteem the less likely you are to indulge in unconscious emotional behaviour. Fewer things will feel threatening, the need to compete wanes. The reverse, poor self awareness, inadequacy and low self esteem mean a much greater dependence on unconscious emotional behaviour.

This may make you into a successful warlord or corporate magnate but it will not make you happy. Unfortunately our ignorance of our own unconscious emotional dilemma means that as parents and as a society we tend to undermine self esteem and self confidence in each other. Our children especially suffer in this respect and so the cycle is perpetuated.

Our self perceptions develop especially in childhood. We absorb them into the unconscious while we are vulnerable and at a time when consciousness has not yet manifested itself. As dependent, vulnerable children, naturally, we are essentially defenceless against this process.

Most of these self perceptions come from interacting with our parents. Most parents are completely unqualified to handle this. They give it little or no conscious thought merely unconsciously, unknowingly, handing down their own flawed conditioned responses and self perceptions.

Take your own childhood for example. At what point did you cease to be an adorable baby and begin to feel the pressure to improve and to conform? Chores, responsibilities, exams and tests, constantly monitoring and assessing those around you, your competitors, and yourself. Gotta be better, smarter, faster.

We behave like that and create our own illusion of reality. Our world seems overwhelmingly real, forcing us to take part, to be complicit in our own misery. It doesn't have to be like this, we actually make it this way, unconsciously.

Why? Because we are taught and believe that we cannot survive alone, we are insufficient and inadequate so we must struggle and compete to measure up. We have to be productive and useful otherwise we will be abandoned. This is the engine room that generates unconscious emotion. It is completely flawed and out of date. An emotional steam engine trying to power a star ship.

However you can't fault Mother Nature's logic. It's very simple, it seemed to work for mum and dad and thousands of previous generations, so it will probably work for little Johnny too. But as we know what works for Mother Nature is survival of the fittest, not happiness and fulfilment. Breathing, yes, but deeply unhappy and tragically unfulfilled and our survival, a coincidence! Would we die without all this unconscious BS, no! Our environment has changed but the unconscious has not, it is unaware of the passage of time.

The cycle of conflict and suffering is completed at the expense of future generations, at the expense of our children and unconsciously endorsed by us. Yes, it is powered by emotion but that same emotion is also a precious resource. By allowing ourselves to feel all our emotions with the intent of examining them we can place our conscious self between emotion and behaviour. We can break the cycle of suffering. We can unravel the source of each emotion and challenge the self perceptions that generate them.

Then we discover the shocking truth, that many of these deeply ingrained beliefs, these core imprints that define us and how we behave are deeply flawed or simply untrue.

How we perceive ourselves, the very marrow of our existence, is built on lies and deceit.

Chapter 4 - The Unconscious

The unconscious mind pre-dates self awareness and intelligence. It is primarily concerned with our physical survival and as such it is very much our default setting. No matter how cultured and sophisticated we think that we are, the unconscious mind is firmly in charge.

The unconscious is the home of emotion. It lurks in the ancient hind brain, a part of the Limbic system, from a time when we still lived in the primal ooze. It's been around a while so it's pretty well dug in.

A threat appears, hair triggered emotion kicks in and behaviour is instantaneous. Behaviour is a reflex, no thought is required. Threat, emotion, action, all in half a heartbeat. This ancient, completely thoughtless system has served us well. Here we stand astride our planet, dominating everything, masters of all we survey, except ourselves!

Jungle or office, there is no difference to the unconscious. The transition to unconscious behaviour is so swift that conscious thought is left playing an endless game of catch up trying to make sense of things, forced to deal with the very real consequences of unconscious emotional behaviour. The unconscious just carries on misbehaving leaving consciousness perpetually fire fighting. We literally don't know what we are doing most of the time. Our unconscious autopilot runs invisible and all powerful behind the scenes leaving us confused, frustrated and unhappy.

Few of us are aware of the unconscious mind and just how powerful a force it is in our lives. As soon as we perceive any kind of threat, real or imagined we instantly revert to unconscious emotional behaviours. Thought, word and deed. I say imagined because in reality most of the things that seem to threaten us are not real threats at all.

When you take the time to examine these threats (I'll show you how,) they turn out to be bogus. Our unconscious misleads, us, keeping us defensive and combative for it's own reasons. A little competitive paranoia is essential in making good gladiators.

Everything and more importantly, everyone, that we encounter, is carefully scanned and threat assessed by our paranoid unconscious. It does not recognise the changes that have taken place in our environment. Remember the unconscious is incapable of conceptualising and time is a concept. The unconscious is unaware of the passage of thousands, millions of years. Yet another of it's failings for things have changed enormously in that time.

The nature of the things that threaten us has also changed. There are no more Sabre Toothed Tigers around. However when our unconscious perceives a modern threat, say a new guy at the office who's smart and good looking, our behaviours, though different, are still fuelled by primordial unconscious emotion.

Insecurity, anxiety, fear of a potential rival, fear of being displaced by a better candidate, all of these emotions well up instantaneous and unbidden. All of this as you are introduced and sit around a conference table together eying each other like "civilised" people.

We don't sniff each other's backsides, stiff legged with our hackles up but it's pretty close. Our unconscious, emotional response to perceived threat **has not** changed for thousands and thousands of years. We are basically primitive in spite of our suits and our degrees.

All of this affects our behaviour without us realising it. We may unfairly decide that we dislike this person. We may undermine, criticise and argue with him. We may seek alliances with others against him. Factions form, a powerful secret unconscious objective evolves, regardless of the groups intended purpose. It's called office politics. He of course, will fight back. The list of possible behaviours is extensive.

No longer acceptable

The basic emotional response remains unchanged. Fear of abandonment born of anxiety and a sense of inadequacy.

If you aren't careful your whole life will be wasted fighting imaginary foes when the real enemy lies within you. I personally spent many years in the corporate jungle fighting tooth and nail, wasting time and energy on, what was for me, a futile, miserable experience. The corporate world seems so real, so absorbing and distracting that most of us can't see past it. It is only when we realise how deeply unhappy we are, usually around middle age, that we begin to wonder.

At this point there seems to be no answer, no alternative so we take a pill and go back to what we know. Perhaps we just weren't trying hard enough and of course by then we are weighed down with responsibilities. Children, partners, mortgages, bills, all very real and hard to ignore. It is all too easy to scoff at new

Appearances can be deceiving

approaches and stay safe within the herd where at least we have a place.

Take Marion for example, she runs her own successful business, she employs eighteen people. A straight "A" student all the way through school, she has her MBA and speaks three languages. She chairs the local Chamber of Commerce and makes large donations to local charities.

Marion is a human dynamo, a workaholic, the epitome of success by society's standards. Public speaking, the gym, marathons, dancing, Marion is the life and soul of the party. She is a driven woman but driven by what?

As a child she was driven relentlessly by her parents. No matter how hard she tried they constantly criticised and pushed her to do better. NOTHING she ever did was good enough to win their approval. This sense of inadequacy is what relentlessly drives Marion but happy, fulfilled, no.

All of this comes from the incorrect perception of our own inadequacy as individuals. This creates a compelling need to compete. This starts as an instinctive terror of being alone. Alone we are doomed, the individual cannot survive without family and tribe. This instinctive fear is re-enforced by the way that we are raised.

We train our children to conform to the needs of the family and of society so that they will fit in with minimum fuss and effort. We train them to strive to be better than they are, unconsciously endorsing within them a false, low perception of their own intrinsic worth. The child becomes even more competitive for fear she won't measure up and so be abandoned. Alternatively the child may become withdrawn and introverted living invisibly in a private world of his own.

This competitive streak affects all our relationships even those within the family. Brothers compete with sisters, husbands against wives. We are physically allied for the purposes of survival but true intimacy is impossible while the (false) threat of abandonment looms. Spiritually and emotionally we are isolated and alone, afraid to be vulnerable. We abandon ourselves to fit in. Ironically, this biological need to herd together keeps us apart on a higher level. It is within this unhappy, unconscious, arena that a thoughtless and cruel mother nature holds court.

People who are relaxed in their own intrinsic value are threatened by very little. They do not blindly compete driven by the need to either dominate or to conceal their own perceived "inadequacy." Such people are rare.

This is the kiss of death to the unconscious world that we inhabit and so without realising it we drive intrinsic value out of our children early. Our children then go on to do the same to their kids. In fact, for a true sense of intrinsic value to exist outside of the nursery it must be consciously rediscovered by the adult in a lifetimes work.

A conscious being

However the reconstructed adult can never again be the child. That new person is a composite of childish innocence, hard won experience and profound self knowledge. A conscious being seeking Enlightenment, more than the sum of her parts.

In this way our seemingly senseless suffering is given meaning, for in coming to terms with it we find our true selves and fulfil our true destiny.

Before that can happen we must first realise how powerful the unconscious is and how we are dominated by unconscious emotional behaviour.

We must not only change our unconscious behaviour, we must first fundamentally change, or rather correct the way that we perceive ourselves as human beings. Much of what we have been conditioned to believe about ourselves is far from true and must be discarded and replaced.

This level of introspection is typically shunned. The emotions generated by the unconscious as a result of even considering self examination are unpleasant and so we tend to avoid them. The Tao Of Emotion can bring *real* change and of course we hate change, we fear change. In book two we will learn how to challenge and examine these emotions.

Emotion is just energy, neither good nor bad. It can feel unpleasant but it cannot directly hurt us. It causes suffering indirectly because we allow it to determine how we behave. The only way to journey beneath emotion and get at the unconscious is to allow yourself to feel and to explore all of your emotions.

In general this is not something that we have any experience of. Not good experience anyway. We are not aware of any structured approach to the problem, although one does exist. We have no skills, no model to follow and no clear idea of what it is that we would be looking for. The whole project seems fraught with danger, it's overwhelming and ephemeral. It's like trying to nail jelly to the ceiling. How can you fight yourself? You don't. As soon as you engage the unconscious in those terms you have lost. Think about it, your fledgling consciousness against millions of years of evolution? An uneven contest to say the least!

That is exactly how your own unconscious mind will distract and frustrate you. It will invite you to compete with it, while it sets the rules and chooses the battle ground. It is the master of conflict, it doesn't even have to win; it just needs you to take part.

You do not fight, you cannot win an open fight; you will always be outnumbered and outgunned. Fighting is not your purpose. You observe and learn as much about your opponent as possible and report back to the main body. We will use the enemy's own force against him, an old martial arts trick. By designating the unconscious

A scout, no longer just a soldier

as a threat we can use our skills against it by treating it as we would an opponent.

The only way to win is not to fight. To use a combative analogy (let's stick with what we know,) you are now graduating from the army to a Special Forces Recon Unit. You no longer engage the enemy directly. Your new role is to use conscious initiative, discipline and training to study your opponent and gather intelligence. You are too valuable to get mixed up in a fire fight.

This is a comfortable, familiar approach for us and allows us to give the intangible unconscious form so that we can become aware of how it effects our behaviour and why.

"Supreme excellence consists in breaking the enemy's resistance without fighting." Sun Tzu.

By learning to understand the unconscious we can retrain it and recruit it to serve our conscious needs. Imagine if every time you were criticised you unconsciously examined your critic for signs of unconscious emotion. Imagine that at the same time you were able to search for truth within this criticism without feeling threatened. This is your new reflex, not anger or fear. You are so practised and expert that the technique has become a part of your unconscious. You simply need to decide to understand and reconstruct your unconscious mind, secure in the deep awareness of your own intrinsic value.

The Tao Of Emotion will provide structure and format for this process. This has all been done before. The truth is you cannot do this by yourself; there are those who can and must help. This is something that we must do together. Our human interactions are not threats, they are opportunities. This is how we build true intimacy.

The unconscious contains a treasure trove of information about you. How you perceive yourself, your self esteem and self confidence and how you relate to the people around you. It will not surrender it's secrets easily. They must be extracted through a fiery wall of your own emotion.

The separate strands of your unconscious have to be teased out and examined for truth. Bad imprints have to be reconstructed, your old perceptions and behaviours interrupted and altered. The unhappy gladiator must be reborn, fit, for life as a self aware, sentient being.

It's no wonder the prospect of such a transition makes us anxious. This is the ultimate in personal responsibility and most of us will avoid it, even when we realise the nature of our dilemma. You have to be in the right place, ripe with suffering, ready to begin the resolution of your own dilemma.

There is no one to blame, God will not do it for you. Your life is a real live epic adventure but will it have a happy ending? Maybe, if you accept the responsibility, you can make it so.

That, is what we're here for.

Chapter 5 - Core Imprints

In order to regulate our behaviour without the need for conscious thought, the unconscious uses a set of behavioural imprints. These unconscious core imprints or beliefs predetermine how we will behave in any given situation. For example when you feel threatened you will behave in a manner typical of you and your individual core imprints.

We all have these core imprints, we are just unaware of them. Their primary function is survival and so speed is of the essence. When the core imprint is triggered, the relevant emotion instantly kicks in with the pre-programmed, unconscious behaviour. For example, at a team meeting Helen feels criticised by Dan; she instantly reacts by getting angry. That anger in turn effects her behaviour *without* her conscious knowledge. She knows that she is angry but she blames Dan for that without understanding that her anger comes from her own core belief of inadequacy, not Dan.

These days behaviours are usually more subtle but no less destructive. Counter criticism, manipulation, undermining, gossiping, back biting and sulking. Passive aggression has been elevated to an art form but the basic emotional response is unchanged. It kicks in instantly when the core imprint of inadequacy is triggered.

Our daily reality becomes choked with these unconscious emotional responses because they have very real consequences. Dan and Helen begin a long and bitter feud. Helen and the boss Elaine are the only women on the team; ultimately Dan is passed over for a well deserved promotion because, thanks to Helen's subtle undermining, he is labelled unfairly as a male chauvinist.

Dan's original comment was actually not a criticism of Helen at all; he was trying to highlight systemic problems that were causing problems for Helen. Helen has a core imprint of inadequacy as a result of a critical parent. Not only is she extremely sensitive to criticism she frequently sees criticism where there is none. Her inadequacy imprint is on a hair trigger.

What makes it worse is that Helen is actually extremely talented and good at her job but because of her inadequacy imprint she can't see it. This devastatingly influential and powerful imprint is based on a lie! Helen is not inadequate; she just believes that she is, without realising it. No conscious thought is involved in any of this.

Pre-dating conscious thought and self awareness this system of core imprints developed from a time when life and death situations were a daily occurrence. However since the unconscious mind is unaware of the passage of time it perceives no difference between that dangerous time and this relatively safe time.

We form these core imprints as vulnerable children based mainly on our interaction with our parents. We do whatever it takes to make up for our seemingly real inadequacy and avoid abandonment.

This extremely effective method of controlling behaviour is inappropriate and damaging for modern, intelligent and self aware people. The trouble is that these imprints operate invisibly. We are unaware of the extent of their influence, as was intended by Mother Nature. Our conscious interference slows them down and makes them ineffective from a survival point of view.

However we no longer live in a deadly environment, unconscious core imprints are not appropriate for sentient beings. It is appropriate and necessary that we should begin the long, painful transition from life as unconscious beings to life as conscious beings. We can learn to do this, we can actively pursue consciousness.

It is crucial that you find out what your core imprints are and how they effect your behaviour on a day to day basis. For complete self awareness you also need to understand the process by which they were formed. Only then, as you discover the lies/untruths upon which they are based will you experience emotional realisation.

This is the tragedy of the unconscious dilemma. Our minute by minute, day to day behaviours are dominated by core beliefs about ourselves that are simply not true. They are purposely designed by Mother Nature to make us combative participants in the survival of the fittest regime that spawned us.

Yet these untrue self beliefs are so deeply ingrained that we are completely unaware of them. We live with the terrible consequences of this ignorance because our unconscious behaviour has consequences that are very real. This is especially true with regard to how we interact together. For example when we feel threatened by someone else we may become aggressive or we may become passive together with a whole range of behaviours that go with these feelings.

Those around us respond in kind, we retaliate and the whole cycle of suffering escalates until it seems completely overwhelming and real. Anger, criticism and blame flare up uncontrollably driven, **not** by our "enemies" but by a basic core belief in our own inadequacy and fear of abandonment. We are addicted to blaming our enemies but actually it is our own untrue core beliefs about ourselves that create the problem and lead us to conflict.

Our unconscious core beliefs generate vast quantities of behaviour all of which has a domino effect that quickly spirals out of our control. Our whole lives become one glorious unconscious mess! This leaves the conscious mind struggling to catch up and make sense of it all. An impossible task since it is merely trying to cope with the symptoms generated by faulty unconscious core imprints. The conscious mind rarely becomes aware of the unconscious core beliefs that generate this blizzard of behaviour.

This is the sandy foundation upon which we attempt to build happy lives for ourselves!

The mere intellectual knowledge of this dilemma is insufficient. You must **feel** the pain and sadness, the gut wrenching truth of how you were unconsciously corrupted and turned into a gladiator. Only then can genuine compassion and self love begin to grow. As it blooms within you and for you, so it will then bloom, like a miraculous flower, for those around you. Suddenly your competitors become your brothers and sisters in arms, human beings who have suffered as you have suffered.

As realisation dawns and the scales fall from your eyes you see only the similarities, even when others attack and undermine you. You begin to see the unconscious at work on yourself and on those around you. At this point you can begin conscious intervention to break the cycle of suffering and restrain your own unconscious behaviours. This will dramatically reduce the unpleasant consequences of unconscious behaviour and vastly improve your life.

The list of these unconscious behaviours is large and very complicated. Passive aggressive, assertive, submissive, there is a whole industry out there dealing with the symptoms of flawed unconscious core beliefs. You could go mad trying to deal with them one by one. It is vital that you understand and are aware of the unconscious core beliefs that generate these behaviours. Otherwise you will get bogged down, confused and overwhelmed in a sea of habitual unconscious behaviour and self analysis.

Although our unconscious behaviours may be much more complex than simple fight or flight the actual underlying core beliefs are relatively few in number and basically simple in nature. The chief culprits are inadequacy and fear of abandonment. I am constantly amazed at how common these two tyrannical imprints are and just how much effort we unwittingly expend under their unconscious influence.

A major problem is the speed at which these imprints operate. Speed means life and death to the unconscious. There simply is no time to think. It believes that thinking could get you killed. That's how the unconscious views things even though this is no longer a valid representation of how we live. These days life and death situations are rare. It is inappropriate and harmful for self aware, semi conscious being to live like this. It makes us miserable and unhappy. The consequences of unconscious emotional behaviour are devastating.

Take suicide for example. No other species will actually take its own life rather than continue living in this unconscious, seemingly senseless emotional chaos.

Every year about a million people commit suicide. That represents an increase of 60% in the last 45 years. Somebody commits suicide every 40 seconds and that number is expected to double by 2020. For every person that kills themselves 20 more attempt suicide. Think of their families, all their friends and acquaintances.

How many more are driven mad with misery and despair? How many die of stress related disease? How many are just plain old unhappy spiralling into addiction, depression and despair? These numbers will get worse until we realise the nature of our conscious/unconscious dilemma.

Remember, this dominant unconscious system in which we exist developed before intelligence evolved, never mind self awareness. The unconscious has no concept of time, it cannot conceptualise. This is your default setting and will continue to be so until you consciously decide to learn the necessary skills and become a more conscious being. This is a shock to those who genuinely realise it. We are not conscious beings we are unconscious beings.

The unconscious is cunning

Crucially it is our unconscious core imprints that dictate how we perceive ourselves, especially in comparison to those around us. How we feel about ourselves and how we interact together as people is determined by our unconscious core imprints. Of course this attitude effects every aspect of the world that we live in.

There's nothing like a sense of your own inadequacy to motivate you to quarrel and compete. Inadequacy is seen by the unconscious as a successful and *necessary* survival technique. After all you have survived, here you are, incontrovertible evidence that inadequacy works. This is the way the unconscious "thinks." **Your own unconscious wants you to feel inadequate!** You will seek inadequacy and be driven by it one way or another. Incredible!

This is a dark deception and a difficult concept to realise. The unconscious is devious and cunning but it is also outdated and full of errors. There is a sequence to these errors. Following the sequence from the beginning helps in realising our unconscious dilemma.

We are all born with the innate terror of being alone. Alone we are weak and inadequate. Without the collective family and tribe we die. A baby will cry when his mother leaves the room for this reason and that primal fear follows us through life. This is the first error, being alone is no longer a significant problem because we never really are.

However the child, incorrectly accepting this ancient, outdated instinct as truth modifies her behaviour to prevent being abandoned by her family. Instead she abandons herself, believing herself to be vulnerable and inadequate alone. She will do anything to fit in with the family's values, whether they are healthy or unhealthy. We all do this.

This self abandonment extends into all her future social interactions. Unconsciously following her core imprint of inadequacy and fear of abandonment she will do what it takes to stay within the group and so survive. This is the second error. Although inadequacy and self abandonment may seem successful, survival is merely coincidental. Self abandonment is too high a price to pay for a coincidence!

This perception of inadequacy has another function. It makes us more competitive. This compounds the third error; that only the strong survive. No longer true!

Even so the child abandons herself and does what is necessary to stay within the family. No matter how twisted or damaging it is preferable to abandonment. Competing with siblings for attention and resources, competing with those around her throughout her whole life, emulating and learning from her emotionally stunted peers.

She will even seek out or faithfully replicate the same "successful" environment in adulthood no matter how abusive or destructive it actually is.

As parents we encourage our children to better themselves, unconsciously endorsing the child's belief that he is not good enough as he is.

"Eat your vegetables or you won't grow up to be big and strong."

"You have to do well at school or you'll end up pushing a brush."

We use our own warped experience and unconscious imprints as the basis for the child's education at home. Schools are no better, exams, tests, homework, hierarchy, competition. All of it re-enforces the child's unconscious belief in his basic inadequacy.

Feeling inadequate and behaving competitively *seems* to work. The child survives. In simplistic, unconscious terms, it makes sense to stay with a good thing. Inadequacy seems good to our warped unconscious! To varying degrees inadequacy and competitiveness extends itself into every aspect of life. Relationships, career, even our physical shape will be effected.

Why is dieting is so difficult? On the face of it it's a simple matter of exercise and diet, unless you have an inadequacy imprint. Then, although your conscious intent is to lose weight, your unconscious desire to stay with the "successful" inadequacy strategy undermines your efforts. You "fail" to lose weight and can then feel inadequate for being fat as well. Of course it must be working, because you survive.

Naturally you would deny this completely if it was suggested to you. You might even feel threatened by the idea and become angry. You may feel like that now, but hold on, it's not a criticism. Does this addiction to inadequacy and being competitive not explain the repetitive, frustrating way that we seem to go around in this endless, repetitive cycle of conflict and suffering?

Intimate relationships are avoided or may be sabotaged. Many married couples spend their whole lives in co-dependent relationships, denying themselves to avoid being alone. The person who feels inadequate may consciously seek an intimate relationship but unconsciously be afraid of being discovered and abandoned. Such a person may seek any excuse to break off the relationship and

We are a mystery to ourselves

blame the other party. Or they may live together as virtual strangers for decades never truly knowing each other.

That person will NEVER accurately portray themselves to a potential partner. To do so is to invite discovery as inadequate and be abandoned and perish. How could they be truly intimate when they simply do not know themselves? Do any of us? We are afraid to look; we think we know what we will find. Why else do we puff ourselves up and exaggerate our status and wealth? Why are we so dishonest when seeking a mate?

A person with a core imprint of inadequacy may feel that they MUST have a partner no matter how unsuitable that partner may be. Somehow they are attracted to the same type no matter how many times they get divorced? It always ends in "failure" because that is the unconscious goal.

By the time we are married and begin to

The comfort of failure

get to really know each other it's too late. My own parents spent forty years together and didn't even like each other much. Children may be involved and of course they emulate their parents and blame themselves for the, these days, inevitable divorce. The cycle of failure and suffering is perpetuated and guess what, we are surviving.

So the addict will often fall off the wagon even after successful detoxification. He will always incorrectly believe himself to be inadequate and unconsciously seek out the comfort of failure.

In fact we are being deceived by our own unconscious mind. The unconscious is programmed to lock us into a competitive cycle of suffering, conflict and failure. Real success would actually inflict incredible stress because then the individual is forced to acknowledge the real self and accept personal responsibility for his own destiny. This is terrifying to most people. We prefer to stay in our familiar self made, hell on earth. This is the devil that we know and are accustomed to. As far as the unconscious is concerned inadequacy is a tried and tested formula for success!

The truth is that we survive in spite of fear of inadequacy and abandonment, not because of it. However the quality of our lives is blighted to such an extent that as a result we are driven to distraction, addiction and even suicide. We **need** to live, not merely survive. This process effects all of us to varying degrees. It does not merely apply to people that we cynically describe as "losers." Some of the most "successful" people in society are driven by their unconscious core imprint of inadequacy.

There is no escape until you realise the nature of the prison in which you exist. Not just intellectually but emotionally. True realisation will normally reduce you to tears. This is not self pity, this is crucial emotional realisation. Once truly realised, the extent of this unconscious deception will blow your world apart!

Inadequacy is a myth, abandonment a fallacy. Two of our most powerful and common core imprints, rigid dogmas that have enslaved us for aeons, turn out to be absolute rubbish when we dare challenge them! The blizzard of unconscious emotional behaviour that results, redundant! It is actually harmful, dangerous and it makes us incredibly unhappy.

What other core imprints do we suffer from? (Please note that I am concentrating on negative core imprints for the purposes of this book, there are positive ones too!)

Each individual must set out to determine what their own imprints are. I can only describe my experience and explain how I went about it.

My unconscious core imprints run like this,

1. Fear of vulnerability
2. Inadequacy
3. Abandonment
4. Annihilation

We are terrified of being alone

I avoid vulnerability/intimacy with people because I feel that they will inevitably discover my inadequacy and then abandon me. I surround myself with a clique of non threatening people as a survival technique (camouflage) but avoid real intimacy with them. My unconscious believes that I will die if I am alone. Within that group I am competitive, manipulative and volatile, desperately trying to maintain or enhance my place in the hierarchy.

That seems ridiculous at first which clearly indicates how far removed we are from the reality of our unconscious. We do not seem to think in terms of life and death but the unconscious does not think, it just is. It is primitive and yet it controls us still.

As motivators these core imprints cannot be understated. They beat all, dwarfing and stunting spirituality, intellect or love.

However the truth is very different. When I allow myself to be vulnerable with people (appropriately,) they respond in kind. We all have these feelings and when someone opens up to us we naturally reciprocate.

I am not inadequate at all. I am creative, dynamic and compassionate. Some people even like me and seek my company! I will not be abandoned and even if I was I would be quite capable of surviving on my own. I certainly will not die as a result. The truth is completely different to the unconscious reality portrayed by my core imprints.

Inadequacy and fear of abandonment may lead me to stay with the family/tribe and seem well integrated, even popular, but true intimacy, never. True intimacy is a threat because then we are discovered and abandoned. This fear keeps us isolated and alone no matter how integrated we seem to be. We are just hiding in plain sight.

Yet these inaccurate imprints seem to be the foundation of my life. They define me as distant, aggressive and unpleasant and fill my life with loneliness and pain but this is not who I really am. The real me still exists buried under layer upon layer of core imprints and life experience. The child within waits in the rubble of her life to be excavated, rescued and reborn.

These unconscious core imprints generate oceans of self replicating pain and suffering on an unimaginable scale. Ironically this suffering unites us since none of us are immune from the blight of inadequacy. It's just a question of degree.

We have so much in common if we could just stop treating each other as rivals for a moment. However that's not likely to happen because all of this is unconscious behaviour. We are not even aware of it or the dreadfully flawed process behind it.

When all is said and done, are we inadequate? Is the child to blame for the emotional poverty and ignorance of his parents? Is he inadequate? No.

We all of us have our gifts, each one a priceless treasure.

So the unconscious is completely **wrong** but for it's own reasons. It has failed to adapt to the world that we live in today limiting us to conflict and suffering. True, there are threats out there but very few of them are serious enough to merit aggressive unconscious intervention. Actually, the worst threat of all is our own unconscious.

It simply cannot keep pace with the rate at which we are consciously evolving. Unconscious evolution took millions and millions of years. The pace of our evolution has made a quantum leap within the last *two hundred years*. The unconscious was only expressed and scientifically recognised one hundred years ago. We have outgrown our unconscious master but it will not free us easily. Consciousness will have to fight for control. We have to fight to free ourselves, or rather; fight to not fight, to free ourselves.

The entire unconscious construct is designed for dumb animals not sentient human beings. Our unconscious core imprints are at odds with who we really are, with who we can be. We must become aware of them and learn to behave consciously if we are to prosper and grow.

It's an uneven contest. The unconscious mind is completely dominant but living unconsciously is, by its very nature and design, an unhappy experience. We want more; we are capable of so much more. Our suffering eventually causes us to question our unconscious state and seek out alternatives. The truth of our inner divinity remains in spite of everything.

If we are to know ourselves and understand the unconscious we must follow our emotions and identify our unconscious core imprints. They must be fully understood and realised intellectually, spiritually, physically and emotionally. Intellect alone will not be enough. The core imprints that we inherit and develop are not based on truth. The child is **NOT** inadequate. We are ignorant and confused yes, inevitably, given our history, but inadequate, no. We will evolve and resolve our human dilemma but it will be hard.

In book two we will go into how to follow emotion and deal with your core imprints. It is important at this point that you focus on realising the truth of what you have just learned **before** you do anything else. Doing is one of our greatest addictions and will be a constant source of trouble on the journey ahead.

Realisation must begin, it must be felt, heart and soul, as well as understood, before the doing begins. Intellect alone will not serve you here, it's a good starting point, especially for the Western mind, but more emotional skills will be needed. The process of realisation will take years, in fact it will never cease. It's an ongoing work in progress and a fundamental piece of who you are.

Chapter 6 - Realisation

If you give these revelations even a little thought, the enormity of it all soon becomes intimidating. Most of our lives are filled with family, relationships, career, all of the hectic paraphernalia of modern life. To suddenly realise that most of this is, as Shakespeare puts it,

"Sound and fury, signifying nought," is a profound shock. To realise that all of this is generated by the unconscious just to keep us distracted and competing in the rat race, well it's upsetting and disturbing.

This new perception means admitting that you, and indeed society, are the victims of a huge deception perpetrated by an unconscious we are barely aware of. I am reminded of the movie, "Matrix". Watch it again from this new perspective and you will realise that it's not a work of fiction at all; it's a metaphor for life. As ever, truth is stranger than fiction.

It's a lot to swallow, look at it as a buffet rather than a snack. Be greedy. You have to keep going back again and again and not be put off by that. Getting it wrong is an integral part of getting it right, it is not failure. The unconscious is quick to label it as such in the hopes that you will give up, clutching gratefully for the comfort of failure, and return to the fold. Society will not recognise or reward your achievements. Just the opposite, society and your desire to belong in it, will be a primary cause of distraction on this journey. Remember, society has been corrupted!

This is a brand new cycle of existence, outside general experience, it runs like this.

1. Awareness of the unconscious dilemma.
2. Desire for change.
3. Being present and open.
4. Identifying truth.
5. Living truthfully.

This new cycle of existence turns everything that we have been taught about success and how to get on in life, upside down. It leaves us feeling exposed and vulnerable, tired, anxious and fearful. The way that we measure success is completely corrupted by an unconscious society wedded to materialism and competition. It's all about the car you drive, the job you do, the house you live in.

In our insecurity and inadequacy we seek to compare ourselves using these corrupted parameters for success. We fail to realise that the unconscious uses all of this to make us competitive. It doesn't care what we drive, only that the "best" of us survive at the expense of those we manage to trample underfoot.

Our lives becomes an all too real maelstrom of self centred competition and strife that consumes our every waking moment draining us of energy denying us the simple pleasures of life. As we flag, foundering and exhausted under the burden of our own illusions, we feel failure nipping at our heels. For lack of an alternative we

Don`t forget to celebrate

redouble our efforts, goaded by a cruel, mindless unconscious.

This process of realisation takes time, ALL that you have. Don't set any limits or pressure yourself. This new self awareness alone is a huge step forward, one that most people never make. Don't forget to celebrate this fact.

The transition to consciousness is an evolutionary path, the work of generations to come. It will easily occupy you for the rest of your days. This is your purpose in life.

So be patient, allow yourself time to adjust, to make mistakes, to give up and then to return and begin again. Realisation is multi layered like an onion. As we peel away each layer a new level of awareness is reached.

You will experience moments of great clarity as well as moments of confusion, uncertainty, anxiety and fear. Bad days and good days, success and failure are all a part of the same process. Black and white, good and bad, Yin and Yang. The good experience is no better or worse than the bad, and both are a part of the whole.

Realisation of the truth doesn't make life any easier but it does give your experience purpose and direction and that is a great comfort. Truth is implacable and once you get a taste for it, you'll be hooked. You cannot un-know truth, it will never let you go. Many people waste their whole lives trying to escape from it. In the process they lose their health, sanity and peace of mind.

You cannot dominate this process or even control it. You can only ever control your own behaviour and sporadically at that. Learn to surrender to the process and do not dwell on the outcome. There is no end, no finishing line, so don't waste time looking for one. You cannot be contained, there is no limit, don't let that frighten you. When fear comes you can learn the skills necessary for dealing with it.

The way to complete realisation is through understanding the mechanisms by which we are controlled by our unconscious. Otherwise you will be effortlessly distracted. In this instance all that the unconscious has to do is work on your fear of change, fear of the unknown fear of being different. In no time you'll be back at work competing harder than ever.

To fully realise the role that your unconscious plays is to realise the role that your conscious self should and must play. This is a vast amount of work, a task fit for sentient human beings. If this doesn't scare you, you're just not doing it right!

Be your own hero

Chapter 7 - What Now?

Many of us have partially realised the nature of the human dilemma. Some come to it via a spiritual path, some through relationship counselling or psychoanalysis, some are just searching. It doesn't really matter how we arrived at this place, it's where we are going that creates such anguish and confusion.

Not really knowing what we are seeking and unsure as to what comes next, we take fright and return to what we know. No matter how unhappy it makes us, we cling to the devils that we know so well.

The lack of a clear path and fear of the unknown cripple us. We lack the basic realisation of our own unconscious dilemma. That is why waking up is the first essential step. Without that cycle shattering realisation and awareness, the unconscious will prevail. It will subtly and discretely undermine our conscious intentions with anxiety and fear of change.

Most of what progress we have made came from the example of great leaders. Buddha, Jesus, Lao Tzu, Ghandi. We follow because it is easier than taking the lead. The thought of taking charge of our own destiny, of being our own leader and hero, fills us with dread. Yet all true teaching will eventually take you to a place where you are alone with yourself, choosing, making the hard decisions, leading.

Regardless of the path that we choose this inevitable and necessary process is crippled by our fundamental lack of self knowledge. In the Tao Of Emotion we realise the nature of our unconscious dilemma. We use our own emotions to unravel the unconscious throwing light and understanding onto the flawed process that spawned and so corrupted our innocence. Only then are we able to rebuild and fulfil our true, limitless destiny.

A clear path and a little company make all the difference and why not? Why go alone? With a little imagination and creativity surely we can come up with a solution?

It's been done before by isolated individuals some of whom paid the ultimate price. We honour them by learning from them and by making our own contribution. Know that there is a way, a process, that it can be done and that this is our purpose.

It will never be easy but we can raise the struggle to general awareness and create a kind of human synergy. We can collectively take humanity's energy and creative genius and bring it to focus on the REAL problems that threaten us, then we will truly have evolved to the next level.

Now, as realisation dawns, recognise the scale of this task. You have the rest of your life and you'll need all of it! The time is yours to spend wisely, there is no need to rush. This is your time, your moment has come. Get ready to shine!

The Tao Of Emotion Book 2

First Steps - will enable you to,

Explore your emotions
Uncover your core imprints
Spot them working within you
Intervene *before* you act
Learn about emotional skills
Anticipate your unconscious as it retaliates
Identify the Truth, seek it, find it, live it

When you buy Book Two receive a free copy of,

Saying No!

Saying No (an audio book narrated by the author) is a look at how we struggle to be ourselves. Learning how to assert yourself consciously is a skill that everyone should possess.

We are either aggressive or take the easy route abandoning ourselves to fit in and please others. Learning to say no is a must if you are going on this trip!

The Tao Of Emotion Book 3

The Long Road - will enable you to,

Surrender to non doing
Cherish the moment
Realise self love
Develop compassion for others
Enjoy the simple things in life

When you buy book three receive the first lesson in Free Your Mind, a course in consciousness, **free.**

www.taoofemotion.com

The Tao Of Emotion

Book One   - Awaken

Book Two   -   First Steps

Book Three - The Long Road

A Course In Consciousness

To find out more and order go to...

...**www.taoofemotion.com** for

Free Audio, video and text downloads.

and,

Libertatii - Get your free subscription to Libertatii, the online magazine, for those who would be free.

www.ingramcontent.com/pod-product-compliance
Lightning Source LLC
Chambersburg PA
CBHW061958040426
42447CB00010B/1811